Taylor's Pocket Guide to

Perennials for Shade

Taylor's Pocket Guide to

Perennials

for Shade

ANN REILLY
Consulting Editor

A Chanticleer Press Edition
Houghton Mifflin Company
Boston

Based on Taylor's Encyclopedia of Gardening, Fourth Edition,

revised and edited by
Gordon P. DeWolf, Jr.

Prepared and produced by Chanticleer Press, New York
Typeset by Dix Type, Inc., Syracuse, New York
Printed and bound by
Dai Nippon, Tokyo, Japan

Library of Congress Catalog Card Number: 88-46141
ISBN: 0-395-51019-8

00 10 9 8 7 6 5 4 3 2 1

CONTENTS

GARDENING WITH PERENNIALS FOR SHADE

PERENNIALS HAVE been called the backbone of the flower garden. Year after year they return, bringing beauty to the landscape in a vast array of colors, shapes, and sizes. Perennials can stand on their own or be combined with shrubs, bulbs, or annuals to create unsurpassed glory in your garden. The perennials in this book have been chosen because they are widely available and relatively easy to grow in a range of shade situations.

What Is a Perennial?

Simply defined, a perennial is a plant that produces flowers for more than one year. Perennials may last for just a few years or for several generations. Although trees and shrubs are technically perennials, the term is generally understood to mean the herbaceous perennials—garden flowers. Most herbaceous perennials die back to the ground each winter, but they have persistent rootstocks that remain alive, and the plants grow back and flower the following year.

First Steps Toward Planting

No other plants are as versatile and offer so much to the gardener as perennials. No matter where you garden, in the country or the city, on a small terrace or an acre of land, in varying amounts of sun or shade, a great many perennials will grow and flourish there. The key to success is to choose the right plants for your environment.

Where Does Your Garden Grow?

Some perennials are so hardy that they can survive almost anywhere; others can live only within certain temperature or humidity ranges. The perennials that you choose must be suited to your garden, whether it is hot or cold, dry or wet.

Plant hardiness is based on three factors: temperature, availability of water, and soil conditions. Of these, temperature is by far the most important. The U.S. Department of Agriculture has devised a map that divides North America into ten zones based on minimum winter temperature (see pages 106–107). Zone 1 is the coldest, with winter lows of −50° F; zone 10 is the warmest, with winter minimums of 30° to 40° F, and is often frost-free. Knowing the zone in which you live is particularly useful when you buy a plant you have never grown before. If the description in this book says "zone 4," it means that the perennial is hardy to zone 4, but will not generally survive winters colder than zone 4.

The zone map is a broad, reliable guideline, but your garden will have a more specific set of conditions, which gardeners call a microclimate. These conditions are the result of location or protection. The north side of the house is often colder than the rest of the garden. It is usually colder at the bottom of a hill or in areas exposed to wind. Warmer conditions exist where the heat of the sun is trapped by a hedge or a fence, or reflected from a pavement.

If you are a beginning gardener, stick with plants that are known to be hardy in your area. After you come to recognize your microclimates, you can experiment with growing a wider range of plants.

How Shady Is Your Garden?

Having to cope with shade is a common problem in mature landscapes, where there are large trees, and in cities where shade is cast by taller buildings. But having a shady yard is no obstacle to having a beautiful garden. All of the perennials in this book will grow in some degree of shade. A number of those that grow in partial shade will also flourish in full sun.

The density of shade—and hence its effect on plants—varies according to the time of day, the time of year, and the source of the shade. Shadows cast by buildings are heavier than those cast by trees, because some sunlight will filter through leaves.

Summer trees in full leaf cast heavier shade than do trees in early spring. There is more daylight during summer in the North than there is during spring in the South, so there is a chance for a fair amount to filter through, even in shady yards.

The term "light shade" is applied to situations where there are up to six hours of sunlight each day, or where there is all-day, lightly dappled shade cast by trees and shrubs. "Partial shade" means four to six hours of sun, or somewhat more heavily dappled all-day shade. "Full shade" means less than four hours of sunlight daily, or heavily dappled shade from nearby trees and shrubs.

If you can choose where to plant your shade perennials, situate them where they will receive morning sun and afternoon shade. Morning sun will dry the dew from the foliage and reduce the chance of disease problems; many plants also benefit if they are spared the hot midday and afternoon sun.

No perennials will flower in dense shade with no direct sunlight at all. If the shade cast by trees is too dense, you can thin out some of the upper branches or remove some of the lower branches to allow more light to reach the garden.

Soil

There are three basic components in garden soil: sand, silt, and clay. If the soil is too sandy, water passes through it rapidly and the soil quickly dries out. Too much clay will trap water, and the soil remains wet and drains poorly. The ideal soil is a mixture of the three components. Most perennials prefer soils that are loamy, well drained, and high in organic matter. Many will survive in poor soil but will grow better if the soil is improved.

The Role of Organic Matter

Good soil contains organic matter, such as peat moss, compost, or leaf mold. A soil that contains adequate amounts of organic matter is said to be rich. Organic matter acts like a sponge to retain water and nutrients, yet permits enough air to pass to the roots of the plants. Organic matter also activates organisms in the soil that break down soil particles and fertilizers to release plant nutrients.

pH

One aspect of the chemical make-up of soil is its acidity or alkalinity, which is described in a ratio called "pH." If the soil is not at its proper pH, certain nutrients are not available to the roots of plants. pH is rated on a scale of 1–14; 7 is neutral, soils from 7–1 are increasingly acid, and from 7–14 are increasingly alkaline.

Although perennials are not overly fussy, most prefer a slightly acid to neutral soil, with a pH of 5.5–7.5. Any exceptions are noted under the individual plant descriptions. Where you live can help determine the pH level of your soil: that in the East and Northwest is generally acid, but the Midwest and Southwest generally have alkaline soil. To be sure, have a sample tested by a soil test lab or your Cooperative Extension Service, or purchase a test kit at your garden center.

If your soil is too acid, add lime to raise the pH; if it is too alkaline, use sulfur to lower it. Many commercial fertilizers are acidic and will lower the pH; peat moss will also lower the pH slightly.

Fertilizer

A complete fertilizer contains nitrogen, phosphorus, and potassium (potash). The amounts of each of these elements present in a fertilizer is described by the three numbers on the package, such as 5–10–5, 10–10–10, or some other formula. The first number is the percentage of nitrogen, the second the percentage of phosphorus, and the third the percentage of potassium. For perennials, be sure to use fertilizer whose second number is equal to or higher than the first number, as too much nitrogen encourages foliage growth at the expense of the flowers. Don't use lawn fertilizers in a flower bed!

Fertilizer can be applied in either granular or liquid form. Liquid fertilizers are generally not as long-lasting and must be applied more often.

Planning Perennial Beds and Borders

Before you actually go outside and start to dig a perennial border or bed, you should plan it on paper. Decide first how large you wish the garden to be. If you are a beginner, start small; you can always add to it later.

A bed is a free-standing garden accessible from all sides. A border is a garden that backs up onto a fence or wall and is accessible from one, two, or three sides. When designing beds and borders, do not make them so wide that you cannot reach into the back or center to tend the plants there.

The shape of the bed or border is determined by the space available, the contour of the site where the light is right, and personal preference. Beds and borders can be any shape— square, rectangular, round, or free-form. Whichever you choose should blend with the style of your home and the rest of the garden.

Designing With Flowers

Select perennials based on their color, size, shape, and blooming period. For maximum effectiveness, it is wise to plan a perennial garden with plants that bloom at different times of the growing season. Study this book or mail-order catalogues before making a final plant list.

If your garden is small, stick with smaller-growing plants. Large gardens can accommodate larger plants, but these will usually look out of place in small gardens. In general, select plants of varying height so that you will have tall material for the back of the border or center of the bed; then medium-sized plants; and lower-growing plants for the front, where they can be seen. (Don't be too rigid, however; this is a flower bed, not a regiment of troops.)

Decide on a color scheme. You can vary this in a perennial garden, choosing, for example, yellow plants for spring, pink plants for summer, and blue and lavender plants for fall. If you want a quiet, reflective garden, choose white, blue, or lavender plants. Red, yellow, and orange flowers are exciting and attention-getting, but they often make the garden look smaller than it is.

Look beyond the flowers to the foliage of garden plants. There may be many months when the plants are not in bloom, but you will still want them to be attractive. Select those with a variety of coarse and fine foliage, and foliage in shades of dark green, lighter green, and blue-green for maximum effect.

When they are new, perennial beds and borders may look sparse; the plants are still small, and some perennials do not bloom the first year. While you are waiting for the garden to grow, you can fill in the spaces with flowering annuals. Annuals can be used in any perennial bed or border, even a mature one, to ensure continuous color and to act as a flowering link between one blooming period and the next.

Buying Plants

You may be lucky enough to have friends and neighbors who will get you started with a few plants, but sooner or later you will want to buy perennials for the garden. These are available at mail-order nurseries and garden centers. Many mail-order nurseries are perennial plant specialists and have a wider selection than you can find in garden centers.

When buying plants at a garden center, look for healthy plants with signs of new growth and no indication of insects or disease. When dealing with mail-order nurseries, rely on experiences that fellow gardeners have had. If you don't know the company, buy only a small amount to "test" them; if they send good plants, you can rely on them in the future.

Planting the Garden

Before you begin work on your garden in spring, you must determine how wet the soil is. Take a handful and squeeze it tightly. If the soil is too wet, it will stick together. Wait a few days and test it again. When it is ready it will crumble. If the soil turns to dust when you do the test, it is too dry; you can either water it or wait for rainfall.

Preparing the Soil

Because perennials live for many years in the same spot, it is worth the effort to prepare the soil well before you plant them. This allows plants to establish good root systems. If you choose to move the plants, well-prepared soil will make it easier to lift and divide them. If possible, prepare soil beds in the fall for planting the following spring to allow the soil to settle and the pH and fertility levels to adjust fully.

To prepare a new bed, first remove any grass or stones in the soil. Turn the soil over with a spade to a depth of 18–20 inches. Next, spread a layer of compost, peat moss, or other organic material over the soil surface, enough so it will make up about 25 percent of the improved soil. If the soil pH needs adjusting, this is a good time to do it. Most garden soils in this country are low in phosphorus, which moves very slowly through the soil. Gardeners usually add superphosphate (0–46–0), at the ratio of 5 pounds per 100 square feet of bed. Add granular fertilizer according to label directions.

Mix all of the ingredients together with a spade or rototiller. Place a sprinkler in the bed for a few hours to settle the soil, and rake it smooth.

Planting the Perennials

If you are planting a new bed, arrange the plants—still in their containers—according to your design and move them around until you are satisifed with the arrangement. If the bed is too wide to reach across without stepping on the newly prepared soil, place a wide board across the bed so you won't compact the soil. Dig a hole for each plant using a hand trowel. If the plants are potted, turn the pot over and hit the bottom to loosen them—never pull a plant out by its stem.

Set the plant in the hole, with the crown about ½ inch above the soil level; it will sink as the soil settles. Firm the soil around the plant with your fingers.

If you are adding plants to an existing bed, determine the location of the new plants to your satisfaction before digging the holes. If it has been a long time since the bed was originally prepared, you may need to add organic matter, fertilizer, and superphosphate and adjust the pH.

If you are planting bare-root plants (that is, plants that do not come pre-potted), soak them in water for 24 hours before planting if the roots appear dried out. Spread the roots out in the planting hole before refilling it with soil.

Whenever possible, do your planting on cool, cloudy days to lessen the chances of transplanting shock. Avoid days that are very hot or windy if at all possible.

Once the plants are in the ground, water them well, carefully soaking each plant at the base. Water the plants regularly, especially if it is hot or dry, until they are established and new growth begins.

Transplanting

The guidelines that apply to planting perennials also apply to transplanting. You can transplant in spring, when growth starts, or—except in areas of extreme cold—in early fall. When transplanting, be sure that you dig up roots as carefully and intactly as possible.

Maintaining the Perennial Bed

Even the simplest of low-maintenance gardens requires some upkeep. Although some tasks may seem unappealing, you will find that your enjoyment of your garden increases in direct proportion to the amount of care you put into it.

Weeding

No gardener can avoid weeding, but you can make the job less time-consuming if you catch weeds when they are young. Weeds will become worse each year if you do not keep on top of removing them. Adding a layer of mulch to the perennial bed also keeps invasive growth in check. Where weeds are a serious problem, spread a sheet of black plastic (available at garden centers) on the soil, punching holes in it so water can pass through, and cover it with an organic mulch of wood chips to camouflage it. If you keep your beds free of weeds, you will be able to remove the plastic in two years.

Fertilizing

Although you added fertilizer at planting time, an application of fertilizer each year afterwards will be necessary. For perennials, use a fertilizer whose second number on the label (phosphorus) is equal to or higher than the first number (nitrogen). Spread the fertilizer on the ground in spring when growth starts or when the plants are in bud. Plants that require heavy fertilizing should be fed when growth starts, in early summer, and eight weeks before the first fall frost. Apply fertilizer to moist soil, and water it in well after application.

Water

In the heat of summer, and through periods of drought, water your plants regularly. Soak them deeply, and avoid getting the foliage wet if possible. If you use a sprinkler or a nozzled hose to water from overhead, do so in the morning. Light waterings, even if frequent, do more harm than good by discouraging deep roots. New plants may require daily watering, especially if it is hot, dry, or windy.

Mulching

A mulch is a protective covering that is spread over soil and around the bases of plants; mulches conserve soil moisture, suppress weeds, and keep the root zone cooler than the air temperature. Mulching also saves work by reducing the need for manual weeding. Apply the mulch thickly, as it will eventually mat down, and avoid placing it too close to plant crowns, where it may encourage diseases and slugs.

When you choose a mulch, consider its availability, cost, appearance, and durability. Organic materials, such as bark chips, leaves, hay, pine boughs, and compost, benefit the soil and are generally preferable to man-made mulching materials. Some mulches will increase the acidity of the soil; others, such as wood chips, may blow around in windy areas and prove a nuisance. Some mulches are potential fire hazards; others may contain weed seeds or diseases that could be transmitted to your plants. If in doubt, describe your situation to your local nursery professional and ask his advice.

Staking

Some perennials produce many stems that tend to flop over if they are not staked. Others are very tall and need support to keep them upright and protected from wind. You can use bamboo sticks, wooden poles, or wire devices similar to tomato cages. When you insert the stake into the ground, be careful not to damage the plant's crown or roots. When tying plants to a stake, use natural twine or twist-ties, and tie loosely so as not to damage the stem.

Pinching and Disbudding

Some gardeners choose to remove a small amount of a plant's growing tip to encourage branching or to modify flowering; this process, known as pinching, can be done with your fingers. Pinch in spring, when the plant is in its most active growth. Plants that are pinched are usually shorter and sturdier than others, and bear smaller but more abundant flowers.

Disbudding, on the other hand, is a method of producing larger flowers. To disbud, remove some of the flower buds in a cluster when the buds are small. The plant will channel proportionately more energy into remaining buds, which will become larger flowers.

Throughout the season, faded flowers and flowering stalks should be removed. Doing so not only improves the appearance of the garden, but also conserves your plants' strength, as they do not expend a lot of energy producing seeds. Additionally, removing faded flowers will encourage some plants to keep blooming or to have a second bloom.

Fall Cleanup and Winter Protection

Taking care of a few small chores in fall will help your plants to have a better winter and a more successful spring. Clean your flower beds of all dead foliage to reduce disease and eliminate areas where insects can overwinter. After the tops of perennials have been killed by frost, cut them back to one inch above the ground; then you will be able to find them the following spring.

After the ground has frozen, use straw, a heavy mulch of leaves, or evergreen boughs to protect newly planted perennials and those with marginal hardiness. The winter mulch is applied to keep plants from being heaved from the ground by alternating freezing and thawing, rather than out of concern for the cold.

Plant Propagation

There are several ways that you can increase the number of perennials in your garden without ordering more plants from your nursery. In general, perennials are increased from seeds, cuttings, and by division of the roots. Many hybrids will not produce flowers "true to type" (that is, just like the parents) from seeds, so it is best to use root divisions or cuttings.

Seeds

You can start seeds indoors or outdoors in flats, or outside in seed beds. Seeds started indoors in flats should be sown in a soilless medium of sphagnum moss and perlite or vermiculite. (Garden soil is not advised as it is heavy and may carry insects and diseases.) Follow instructions on the seed packet. Seedlings require intense light to grow indoors. If you do not have sunny windowsills, grow them under fluorescent lights.

Seeds started indoors will need to be "hardened off" before they can be transplanted into the garden. Move the flats outdoors into a permanent location. You can tell if a cutting has rooted by gently tugging at the stem. If it resists, it is rooted.

Division

When plants become too large or when the amount of bloom decreases, it is time to divide them. In colder areas, it is best to divide in spring; in mild areas, divide in spring or fall.

To divide perennials, carefully lift the entire clump from the ground with a shovel or spade. Some plants may be divided by hand; others may need the assistance of a trowel, spade, or digging fork. Be sure there are signs of growth or growth buds on each division. After the plants are divided, replant them as you would a new plant. If you are sharing your divisions with friends, be sure to place the roots in a plastic bag to keep them from drying out.

Cold Frames

Many gardeners find cold frames useful and versatile, although it is quite possible to garden without one. A cold frame is an unheated, bottomless box with a top of a transparent material such as glass, plastic, or Fiberglas that can be opened or removed. The transparent top admits light and traps warmth in the box.

You can buy a cold frame or make one using wood and an old storm window. Situate it facing south, in an area protected from wind, where soil drainage is excellent.

Cold frames are used to store young seedlings, cuttings, or divisions that are not mature enough to withstand winter. In spring, plants can be moved outdoors to the cold frame before it is warm enough to place them in the ground. Open the frame on warm, sunny days and close it again at night.

Garden Implements

There is no need to spend a fortune for your gardening tools; it is important, however, to have a few of the right tools at hand. It is wise to buy well-made implements, even though they may be more expensive, and to treat them with care. Cheap tools will break very easily. Clean your tools regularly, and don't leave them lying around in the rain or out in the yard over the winter. Set aside a small spot for them in your garage or basement, or put a few hooks and a shelf on an inside wall next to your back door. The basic tools for beginning gardeners are:

A **spade**—not to be confused with a round-point shovel—has a straight blade and a D-shaped handle. It is essential for bed preparation.

A **hand trowel** is the chief tool used in planting. Buy one with a solid shaft.

A **steel rake** is used for leveling the soil after bed preparation.

A **three-pronged cultivating fork** will be necessary for weed control and bed cultivation.

A Note on Plant Names

The common, or English, names of plants are often colorful and evocative: Dutchman's-Breeches, Jack-in-the-Pulpit, Monkshood. But common names vary widely from region to region—Marsh Marigold and Cowslip are both names for the same plant. Sometimes, two very different plants may have the same or similar common names, as with Sweet William and Wild Sweet William. And some have no common name at all. But every plant, fortunately, is assigned a scientific, or Latin, name that is distinct and unique to that plant. Scientific names are not necessarily more right, but they are standard around the world and governed by an international set of rules. Therefore, even though scientific names may at first seem difficult or intimidating, they are in the long run a simple and sure way of distinguishing one plant from another.

A scientific name has two parts. The first is called the generic name; it tells us to which genus (plural, genera) a plant belongs. The second part of the name tells us the species. (A species is a kind of plant or animal that is capable of reproducing with members of its kind, but genetically isolated from others. *Homo sapiens* is a species.) Most genera have many species; *Iris,* for example, has more than 150. *Iris cristata,* the Crested Iris, is a species included in this book.

Some scientific names have a third part, which may be in italics or written within single quotation marks in roman type. This third part designates a variety or cultivar; some species may have dozens of varieties or cultivars that differ from the species in plant size, plant form, flower size, or flower color. Technically, a variety is a plant that is naturally produced, while a cultivar (short for "cultivated variety") has been created by a plant breeder. For the purposes of the gardener, they may be treated as the same thing. *Polygonum bistorta* 'Superbum' is one example.

A hybrid is a plant that is the result of a cross between two genera, two species, or two varieties or cultivars. Sometimes hybrids are given a new scientific name, but they are usually indicated by an × within the scientific name: *Symphytum × uplandicum,* Russian Comfrey, is a hybrid in this book.

Organization of the Plant Accounts

The plant accounts in this book are arranged alphabetically by scientific name. If you know only the common name of a flower, refer to the index and turn to the page given.

Some accounts in the book deal with a garden plant at the genus level—because the genus includes many similar species that can be treated in more or less the same way in the garden. In these accounts, only the genus name is given at the top of the page; the name of the species, cultivar, or hybrid pictured is given within the text.

One Last Word

These are the basic bits of information that you will need to know when starting your perennial garden. There is just one more very important bit of advice: remember that your garden is meant to be a source of beauty and delight. So, above all, don't forget to have fun.

Perennials for Shade

Monkshood *(Aconitum)*

Zones 3–5

Several members of this genus make showy garden plants and are a good source of blue flowers in the late summer and early fall garden. The flowers are 1–2 inches high and bloom in spikes at the ends of the stems. The plants received their name from the large sepal that covers some of the petals and looks like the hood of a monk's habit. The most common species grown are *Aconitum* × *bicolor,* which has flowers sometimes tinged with white, *A. carmichaelii,* and *A. napellus;* all grow to 3–4 feet tall. All monkshoods produce a poisonous juice; *A. napellus* is the source of the drug aconite. Do not grow these plants if you have small children who may eat the leaves or flowers.

Growing Tips

Monkshood prefers cool to moderate climates and a spot in partial shade where the soil is rich, moist, slightly acidic, and well drained. Because the stems are weak, the plants will usually need staking. They rarely need dividing, but when they do, move them carefully, because they resent transplanting.

Red Baneberry *(Actaea rubra)*

Zone 4

Baneberry is a useful plant for the wild or woodland garden. In mid- to late spring, the white flowers bloom in somewhat wispy, erect, 1- to 1½-inch clusters; they are followed in fall by clusters of bright cherry-red berries on a very slender stalk. The berries are poisonous to humans, but birds and small animals consume them. The plant reaches a height of 1½–2 feet and is clothed in bright green, compound leaves that are heavily clefted and toothed. There is a baneberry with white berries *(Actaea pachypoda)*.

Growing Tips

Baneberry likes partial to full shade and a soil that is fertile, rich, moist, and neutral to slightly acid or slightly alkaline. The plant can be divided in late fall or early spring if it becomes overcrowded. Space new plants 18 inches apart. Mulch with a thin layer of leaves to provide extra organic matter and keep the soil cool.

Ladybells *(Adenophora confusa)*

Zone 4

With their handsome blue flowers, Ladybells are very similar in appearance to the closely related bellflowers, of the genus *Campanula*. Ladybells bear drooping, bell-shaped, ¾-inch blue or purple flowers that bloom in mid- to late summer. The plants grow to 3 feet; the flowers appear on thin spikes atop low clumps of 3-inch-wide toothed leaves.

Growing Tips

Ladybells will grow happily in full sun or in partial shade. Average garden soil should provide sufficient nutrients, but be certain it is kept moist and well drained. Space plants 12–18 inches apart. These plants do not like to be moved or divided, so select their permanent homes with care.

Amur Adonis *(Adonis amurensis)*

Zone 4

This perennial rock garden plant, a member of the buttercup family, grows 12 inches high and is clothed in attractive, dark green to purple, fernlike leaves. The golden, cup-shaped to daisylike flowers are 2 inches across and bloom in sprays in early spring, often when there is still snow on the ground. There is also a double-flowered form.

Growing Tips

Grow Adonis in partial shade to full sun; like most family members, it does best in sandy, rich, well-drained soil. Divide the fibrous roots in late spring when flowering is completed and replant 6 inches apart. By midsummer, Adonis will be dormant and the foliage will disappear, so situate it near other plants that will fill in the empty space for the remainder of the season. For best effect, plant in groups.

Bugleweed *(Ajuga reptans)* Zone 3

Bugleweed is one of the best perennials to grow under trees and shrubs, especially if those larger plants bloom at the same time in spring. The rosettes of foliage at the base of the Bugleweed plant are dark green, and each oblong leaf is 2–4 inches long. Spikes of blue to purple flowers 3–6 inches high appear in mid-spring. The plants send out runners that root and produce new plants at their ends. The variety *alba* has white flowers; *atropurpurea* has bronze foliage and blue flowers; *metallica crispa* has metallic, crisped leaves and blue flowers. 'Burgundy Glow', the variety seen here, has variegated foliage with tones of green, white, pink, and purple.

Growing Tips

Bugleweed grows best in partial shade, although it will tolerate full sun in cool climates. It is easy to grow in any well-drained, moist garden soil. It is easily increased by division or by rooting the plantlets that grow at the ends of the runners.

Lady's-Mantle *(Alchemilla mollis)*

Zone 4

For many gardeners, the velvety, silver- to gray-green foliage of Lady's-Mantle provides reason enough to cultivate this plant, which grows in spreading, mounded clumps. The feathery sprays of small, yellow-green flowers that bloom in late spring and early summer are also attractive. The flowers appear in 2- to 3-inch clusters on 12- to 15-inch stems. In warm climates, Lady's-Mantle is an evergreen.

Growing Tips

Lady's-Mantle prefers partial shade; it will grow in full sun only in cool climates. It is very easy to grow in ordinary garden soil but likes a rich, moist soil in hot or dry climates. Keep the plant well watered during periods of high heat. Remove flowers as they start to fade to prevent the plant from reseeding, for it can be invasive if not checked. Divide when plants become overcrowded.

Blue Star *(Amsonia tabernaemontana)* Zone 4

This delicate-looking perennial is aptly named for the blue, star-shaped flowers that bloom in clusters atop stems that grow 2–3 feet tall. Appearing in late spring, the 1-inch cluster is made up of hairy flowers, each but ⅓ inch across. The stems are covered with narrow, pointed, willowlike leaves. The foliage remains tidy-looking throughout the summer and turns yellow in the fall. The plant is also known as Willow Amsonia, and may be sold as *A. salicifolia* (from the Latin for "willow-leaved").

Growing Tips

Grow Blue Star in a cool, moist place in partial shade. Soil should be rich, and mulched to keep it cool and moist. Blue Star does well in very moist soils and will grow well by the water's edge. Soil that is too fertile will lead to loose, open growth. If this happens, cut down on fertilizer and cut the stems back by one-half to encourage a denser habit. Space plants 18 inches apart; divide in spring or fall when they become overcrowded.

Italian Bugloss *(Anchusa azurea)* Zone 4

The small, delicate flowers of the Italian Bugloss are ½ inch across, but the plant is robust and large, growing 3½–5 feet tall. The bright blue flowers resemble oversized forget-me-nots and bloom in graceful clusters during the summer. The foliage and stems are hairy. The variety 'Little John' has deep blue flowers and grows 12–18 inches high; 'Lodden Royalist' is 3 feet high and has royal blue flowers; 'Dropmore' is the most popular of the tall varieties.

Growing Tips

Italian Bugloss is easy to grow in partial shade or full sun in any ordinary garden soil. Its chief requirements are deep watering during dry periods and excellent drainage in winter. Most varieties, except the dwarf ones, require staking. After flowering, cut back the stalks to encourage a repeat bloom and to remove the foliage, which becomes unattractive. Plants are easily divided and self-sow rapidly. Space new plants 18–24 inches apart.

Anemone *(Anemone)*

Zones 4–6

Also known as windflowers, these popular plants are available in many colors and sizes. For the shaded late-spring garden, *A. sylvestris,* the Snowdrop Windflower, is a good choice; it grows 12–18 inches tall and is topped with fragrant, 2-inch-wide white flowers. 'Snowdrops' is a well-known cultivar. For the fall garden, plant Japanese Anemone *(A. × hybrida),* which grows from 1–5 feet tall, depending on the cultivar; the one seen here is 'Robustissima'. *A. × hybrida* has pink or white flowers, 2–3 inches across. Snowdrop Windflower is the hardier of the two species.

Growing Tips

Anemones like partial shade and rich, moist, well-drained soil. Japanese Anemone should be planted in a spot protected from the wind. Both kinds should be divided in the fall; plant the divisions 18 inches apart. Japanese Anemone grows more rapidly and will need division more frequently.

Columbine *(Aquilegia)*

Zones 4–5

Grown in rock gardens and wildflower gardens, columbines are easy to care for and have attractive, spurred, nodding flowers that are often two-toned. One of the most common species is *A. caerulea,* Rocky Mountain Columbine (shown here), which is 2–3 feet tall and has 2-inch-wide blue and white flowers. *A. canadensis,* the Common Columbine, is also widely popular; it grows 1–2 feet tall and has 1½-inch flowers of yellow and red. Both do well in partial shade. There are many hybrids that grow 1–3 feet tall and have 2-inch flowers of red, yellow, blue, white, or purple. Columbines bloom in late spring or early summer and have compound, lobed, dull gray-green leaves.

Growing Tips

Columbines prefer partial shade, which will also prolong the blooming period, but they will grow in full sun where it is cool. Soil should be rich, sandy, and well drained, with a pH between 5.0 and 8.0. Keep plants well watered during growth. They are not long-lived but can be grown easily from seed.

Jack-in-the-Pulpit *(Arisaema triphyllum)* Zone 4

Growing to 1–3 feet, this popular plant is best used in the shaded woodland or wildflower garden. The flower ("Jack") appears in late spring to early summer on a cylindrical spike; it is contained within a green or purplish striped spathe (the "pulpit"), which curls over and hides it. After the flowers fade and the spathe dries up, clusters of red berries appear. The fleshy taproots are edible but very bitter; cooking gives the roots a milder taste, and they were formerly a staple in the diets of certain native Americans.

Growing Tips

Because Jack-in-the-Pulpit is a woodland plant, it must have a rich, moist, cool, slightly acid soil and partial to full shade. It will not grow well where summers are hot. The berries are usually produced only if the soil is quite moist and top-dressed with compost each year. Jack-in-the-Pulpit can be propagated from root divisions in the fall or by seeds.

Goatsbeard *(Aruncus dioicus)*

Zone 4

Goatsbeard is a shrubby perennial growing 4–6 feet tall and wide. The creamy white flowers, each only ⅛ inch wide, bloom in graceful, open, almost wispy 6- to 10-inch panicles (open clusters) in early summer. Goatsbeard is equally effective at the back of the flower border or grown as a single specimen. There are separate male and female plants; the male flowers are more showy, but only the female sets seeds. The variety 'Kneiffii' has finer cut foliage and grows more slowly, reaching only 2–3 feet in height.

Growing Tips

In addition to partial shade, Goatsbeard likes a soil that is rich and moist. The plant does not grow well in extreme heat. Division is rarely necessary, and Goatsbeard does not transplant well; thus gardeners should select its site with care so that the plant will not become crowded or need to be moved.

Wild Ginger *(Asarum)*

Zones 4–5

This fast-growing, spreading, deciduous or evergreen perennial is one of the best ground covers for deep shade. The aromatic leaves are shiny, leathery, and heart-shaped. The bell-shaped flowers are small, just ½–1 inch across; purple to brown, they are often hidden by the foliage in late spring and summer. Common species include *A. canadense,* Canadian Wild Ginger, which grows 6–8 inches high and is deciduous, and *A. europaeum,* European Wild Ginger, an evergreen that grows 7 inches high but is not as hardy as the Canadian.

Growing Tips

Full shade is a must for these plants, as is slightly acid to neutral soil that is rich, moist, and well drained. Space plants 8–12 inches apart; divide in spring or fall.

Asphodel *(Asphodeline lutea)*

Zone 6

According to the mythology of ancient Greece, this plant, which is also called King's Spear, was believed to cover the Elysian fields—the afterworld of happy souls. In the early summer, Asphodel bears fragrant, star-shaped yellow flowers, 1 inch across, that bloom in 12- to 18-inch spikes on stems 2–4 feet tall. The very narrow leaves, which cluster at the base of the plant, resemble blue-green blades of grass.

Growing Tips

Asphodel will grow nicely in partial shade and average, well-drained garden soil. Divide the thick rootstocks in fall or spring when necessary. The plant may need protection in winter in more northerly areas.

.be *(Astilbe)*

Zone 5

When a pretty border or accent plant is needed for partial shade, astilbe is an excellent choice. Erect, feathery plumes of tiny pink, white, or red flowers bloom over fernlike, divided leaves, which are attractive even when the plant is not in bloom. The varieties with white or pink flowers are more vigorous in growth than the reds. *A.* × *arendsii,* which has branched, airy flower clusters reaching a height of 2–3 feet, blooms in early summer. *A. chinensis,* which grows 12 inches high and has denser spikes of magenta flowers, blooms in late summer. *A. tacquetii,* which has thick plumes of magenta flowers, blooms in midsummer; the cultivar 'Superba' is seen here.

Growing Tips

Astilbe prefers partial shade and tolerates full shade. It likes rich, moist soil, but will withstand dry conditions. Astilbes are heavy feeders and benefit from additional fertilizer during the summer. In ideal conditions, they grow quickly and can be divided easily every 3 years. Space new plants 18 inches apart.

False Rockcress *(Aubrieta deltoidea)* Zone 5

A colorful early spring bloomer, False Rockcress is popular as a mat-forming plant for edgings, rock gardens, borders, and ground covers. The plant grows to 6 inches in height; its hairy evergreen leaves are smothered in early spring with ¾-inch flowers of lavender, purple, or pink, which bloom in clusters at the ends of the stalks.

Growing Tips

False Rockcress likes partial shade and light, well-drained soil. Cool, moist growing conditions are a must; it will not grow where summer temperatures are high. Mulch the soil to retain coolness and moisture. If plants are sheared back after they finish blooming, they will be more compact and may have a second bloom in the fall. Plants can be increased by spring division; space new plants 6–8 inches apart.

enia *(Bergenia)* Zone 3

These perennial herbs are grown in borders for their ornamental foliage and very early blooming flowers. There are many hybrids to choose from, with purple, pink, white, or red blossoms; the one seen here is 'Margery Fish', which grows from 12–18 inches tall and bears pink flowers ¼–½ inch across. A commonly cultivated species is Heartleaf Bergenia *(B. cordifolia)*, which has dark green, wavy, heart-shaped leaves. The thick and fleshy foliage forms dense clumps at the base of the plant, and turns purple or red in fall. All are sometimes sold under the name *Saxifraga*, a close relative.

Growing Tips

Plant bergenia in partial shade. It will tolerate full sun only in areas that are cool or have high humidity and rainfall. Rich soil is preferred, but it will do well in poor, dry soils. Wind can tear the leaves, so select the location in the garden carefully. Bergenia can be divided when it becomes crowded.

Siberian Bugloss *(Brunnera macrophylla)* Zone 4

With each successive year, the Siberian Bugloss bears ever-larger foliage. When plants are young, the dull, dark green, hairy leaves are quite small, but eventually they reach 8 inches across. Some varieties have foliage that is spotted or edged in creamy yellow. The small, starlike, bright blue flowers that appear in mid-spring look like forget-me-nots and bloom in airy sprays on 15- to 18-inch stems.

Growing Tips

Plant Siberian Bugloss in partial to full shade. If the plant receives too much sun, the leaves will become scorched. Moist, cool, acid soil is best, although the species tolerates drought. Divide in spring if the plants become too crowded at the base. Siberian Bugloss easily reseeds; the seedlings can be lifted and spaced 12 inches apart.

Calceolaria *(Calceolaria)*

Zone 7

A member of a large group of tropical American plants, Calceolaria can be grown successfully in the garden where summers are cool and winters are mild. These dwarf, tufted plants with irregular flower clusters are known collectively as slipperworts. The cultivar shown here, 'John Innes', bears bright yellow flowers ½–1 inch long, with 2 lips—the upper one small and somewhat pouchlike, the lower one inflated and slipper-shaped. Flowers appear in early summer.

Growing Tips

Plant Calceolaria 'John Innes' in partial shade where the soil is moist and well drained. Propagation may be done by seeding: sow seeds in May, and place pots in a cold frame in June for flowering plants the following year. Propagation by division, which should be done in spring, is an easier method.

Cowslip *(Caltha palustris)*

Zone 4

Also widely known as Marsh Marigold—for its bright golden flowers, rather than any relationship to the true marigolds—this species blooms in the wild throughout much of North America. Its flowers, 2 inches wide, appear in spring; these blossoms actually have no petals, but instead petal-like sepals. The plant grows 1–2 feet high. The most popular variety is 'Flore Pleno', which has double flowers. It is used in shady wildflower gardens and alongside streams and ponds.

Growing Tips

Plant Cowslip in partial shade. As its other common name suggests, the plant is most at home in rich, moist, even boggy, soil. Divide in spring if the plant becomes crowded at the base and plant the divisions 12–24 inches apart.

Bellflower *(Campanula)*

Zones 3–4

Bellflowers are an important group of plants grown primarily for the bright blue flowers of most species, although there are many attractive white forms available. Some members of the group are comparatively low-growing; these include the Carpathian Harebell *(C. carpatica),* which is 6–12 inches high, and the Serbian Bellflower *(C. poscharskyana),* which is a sprawling plant 4–6 inches tall. Shown here is the Great Bellflower *(C. latifolia),* one of the taller, more erect species, which grows to 2–4 feet. The Peach-leaved Bellflower *(C. persicifolia)* reaches 2–3 feet. All start to bloom in early summer; Peach-leaved and Serbian bellflowers will bloom again if spent flowers are removed.

Growing Tips

Bellflowers may be grown in partial shade or in full sun. Most prefer rich, moist, well-drained soil; Serbian Bellflower does best in sandy soil. Stake taller species. Some winter protection will help prevent the crowns from rotting. Divide every 3–5 years in the spring.

Leadwort *(Ceratostigma plumbaginoides)* Zone 6

A fast-growing plant with deep blue flowers, Leadwort forms a mat 6–12 inches high. The tubular, 5-lobed flowers appear in late summer to fall; after they bloom, the large, hairy leaves turn red. (In warm climates, however, Leadwort is an evergreen.) This plant makes a good ground cover for shady places and also does well in a rock garden. It is often mislabeled as *Plumbago larpentae.*

Growing Tips

This species prefers partial shade. Fertile, well-drained soil is best, but the plant will tolerate poor, dry soil, and it is also heat tolerant. In the spring, Leadwort starts to grow very late, sometimes causing beginning gardeners to think it has died; be careful not to plant something else on top of your slow-starting Leadwort. Winter protection is needed in the northern limits of the plant's hardiness zone.

Pink Turtlehead *(Chelone lyonii)*

Zone 4

Pink Turtlehead is valuable in the garden chiefly for two reasons. First, it is a tall plant, reaching 4–5 feet, and is useful in the background of many flower beds. Second, this species blooms in late summer and early fall, when there are few other perennials in bloom, and when summer color from annuals has started to fade. The plant's odd common name comes from the resemblance of the flowers to a turtle's head. The foliage, although bitter, is reportedly sometimes used in making tea.

Growing Tips

Pink Turtlehead needs partial shade and rich, reasonably moist soil. It grows well in swamps or alongside ponds and streams, slowly forming into a large clump, which can be divided easily. Plant the divisions 18 inches apart.

Chrysogonum *(Chrysogonum virginianum)* Zones 5–6

For a long-blooming carpet of delicate, golden color under trees and shrubs, Chrysogonum is a good choice. Also called Golden Star, it blooms from late spring to summer and grows well in the woodland garden. The plant reaches 4–12 inches in height; its hairy leaves are often tinged with purple. The 5-petalled yellow-gold flowers are 1½ inches across.

Growing Tips

This native North American flower is really a woodland species. Plant Chrysogonum in partial to full shade in rich, well-drained soil. It flowers best during cool summers and where the soil is kept constantly moist. In the northern limits of its hardiness, it will need winter protection. Plants may be divided in either spring or fall, and the divisions planted 12 inches apart.

Snakeroot *(Cimicifuga)*

Zones 3–4

Also known as bugbanes, these plants are tall, showy, summer-blooming perennials that are well suited either to the shady border or the wildflower garden. Dense, cylindrical or pointed flower spikes appear in summer over compound foliage. Each tiny white flower has many prominent stamens, which are the major part of the bloom. Black Snakeroot *(C. racemosa)* is quite tall, reaching 6 feet, and has a branched flower spike in midsummer. Kamchatka Bugbane *(C. simplex)*, shown here, is 3–4 feet tall and bears flowers on unbranched spikes in late summer or fall. The plants have an odor that repels insects—hence, "bugbane"—but the odor does not generally create a problem in the garden.

Growing Tips

Members of the genus prefer partial shade and a rich, acid to neutral soil that is kept well watered. These species are slow to develop and should not be disturbed once they are planted. If the shade is too deep, the flowers will not bloom well. Taller types may need to be staked.

Tube Clematis *(Clematis heracleifolia)* Zone 4

Many gardeners think of *Clematis* as a genus of showy vines, but there are several species that are shade-loving perennials. These, too, have showy flowers. The Tube Clematis grows 3–4 feet tall; its fragrant blue flowers, hairy and 1 inch across, bloom in midsummer. The most commonly grown variety is *davidiana,* seen here, which is taller and has deeper blue flowers. The blooms generally appear in loose clusters and look like hyacinths.

Growing Tips

Tube Clematis performs best in partial shade, although it will take full sun if the climate is cool. Soil must be slightly acid, fertile, cool, and moist, but neither excessively wet nor too dry. Mulch in the spring to keep the soil cool. Organic matter should be added to the soil in liberal amounts before planting. The plants like to sprawl, but staking will keep them growing upright.

Lily-of-the-Valley *(Convallaria majalis)* Zone 4

Well known for its delightful fragrance, Lily-of-the-Valley tolerates heavy shade and can be grown under dense trees very successfully. Plant these flowers near your windows or walkways to enjoy the fragrance fully when they bloom in mid-spring. The nodding, bell-shaped blooms that appear along one side of the stems also make excellent cut flowers. Unfortunately, the upright, pointed leaves that grow from the base of the plant can become unattractive by midsummer; during the winter, they disappear completely.

Growing Tips

Plant Lily-of-the-Valley in partial or full shade in moist, rich, fertile, well-drained soil. The roots, which are known as "pips," can be dug in very early spring and kept out of the ground for several weeks before you replant them.

Yellow Corydalis *(Corydalis lutea)*

Zone 5

Because the stems of Corydalis are somewhat weak, these plants often sprawl along the ground. Yellow Corydalis does well in a rock garden, where it can grow over and between the rocks. The lobed leaves may be green or blue-green; they sometimes give a lacy appearance in the flower border. The plants grow to 12 inches tall; the flowers measure ¾ inch across. Bloom occurs during spring and early summer.

Growing Tips

Yellow Corydalis prefers partial shade, although it can be grown in full sun. The soil should be rich, moist, and well drained. It self-sows readily, but the seedlings are not easy to transplant. These plants often die to the ground in the heat of midsummer, so be prepared to plant some annuals in their place to avoid bare spots.

Dutchman's-Breeches *(Dicentra cucullaria)* Zone 4

Fancifully named for its unusual pantaloon-shaped white blossoms, which appear in mid-spring, Dutchman's-Breeches has deeply cut, feathery, pale green leaves. The flowers, which grow to ¾ inch in length, are borne on a stalk 5–8 inches long. The plants grow to 12–18 inches. This species is the most truly shade-loving *Dicentra*.

Growing Tips

Dutchman's-Breeches prefers full shade and should be placed where it is protected from the wind. Even so, the plant often yellows and dies to the ground during the summer. The soil should be fertile, moist, neutral to alkaline, and rich in organic matter. When the plant dies back, it may be cut off and the area filled in with a shade-loving flowering annual. If the plants are crowded, you may wish to divide them in early summer, after the blooming period is finished.

Bleeding Heart *(Dicentra)*

Zones 3–4

The bleeding hearts, with their deep pink to red heart-shaped flowers that bloom on arching or semi-erect branches, are favorites of the partially shaded wildflower garden. Common Bleeding Heart (*D. spectabilis,* seen here) has bold, lobed foliage and blooms in mid-spring; it grows to 2–3 feet. Fringed Bleeding Heart *(D. eximia)* has more finely cut foliage, smaller flowers, and blooms from spring throughout the summer. It is also lower growing, reaching just 1–2 feet in height. There are hybrids of *D. eximia* and *D. formosa* that have finely cut foliage and loose racemes of flowers. These include 'Luxuriant', with dark pink flowers, and 'Bountiful', with red flowers.

Growing Tips

Bleeding hearts are grown in partial shade in rich, moist, slightly acid soil. The foliage of Common Bleeding Heart will turn yellow after the bloom period is finished; the plant may be cut back and the area filled with flowering annuals for a tidier look. All may be divided in early spring when they become crowded.

Foxglove *(Digitalis)*

Zone 4

The source of the heart stimulant digitalis (which is highly toxic if improperly administered), foxgloves are valued in the garden for the tall spikes of bell-shaped flowers that bloom in late spring. Yellow Foxglove (*D. grandiflora,* seen here) has yellow flowers spotted with brown. It grows to 3 feet tall. Common Foxglove, *D. purpurea,* has many hybrids with flowers of white, pink, or purple. It reaches 2–4 feet in height.

Growing Tips

Grow foxglove in partial shade in rich, moist soil. Drainage must be excellent during the winter. Common Foxglove is a biennial but will act as a perennial if the plant is allowed to reseed. All foxgloves reseed freely, but this tendency can be eliminated by cutting the flowers off as soon as the bloom is finished. The plants may also be divided in spring or fall. The tall-growing forms may need to be staked.

Fairy-Bells *(Disporum flavum)*

Zone 4

The pretty, inch-long yellow flowers of Fairy-Bells bloom in spring on 2- to 3-foot-tall plants; the blossoms are set off by shiny, leathery leaves that are attractive all season. This member of the lily family has creeping rootstocks and will spread rapidly to form a large clump for the woodland garden. There are several species that are found in the wild, and a variety, *D. sessile* 'Variegatum', or Variegated Japanese Fairy-Bells, with handsome green-and-white foliage.

Growing Tips

One of the few plants that does well in dry soil in partial or full shade, Fairy-Bells likes rich, well-drained soil. It may need frequent dividing to keep it small; this task should be performed in the spring. Space new plants 2 feet apart.

Common Shooting-star *(Dodecatheon meadia)* Zone 5

The shooting-stars are a group of charming wildflowers native to North America; a few have proved useful in cultivation. Shown here, the Common Shooting-star bears pretty, drooping flowers of white, pale pink, or lilac that look like stars streaking through the sky. The flowers bloom in clusters in late spring; they are borne on leafless stems, 1–2 feet tall, above a basal clump of wavy leaves. The foliage dies down by mid- to late summer.

Growing Tips

Plant Common Shooting-star in partial shade in rich, sandy soil that is high in organic matter; the soil may be acid to slightly alkaline. The plant needs heavy watering during the growing period but must have dry conditions when it is dormant; water left standing in the crown over the winter can be fatal. Common Shooting-stars can be easily divided in the spring after flowering is complete. In the colder areas of its hardiness regions, this species will need winter protection.

Leopard's Bane *(Doronicum cordatum)* Zone 4

In early to mid-spring, Leopard's Bane blooms, bearing clusters of single, bright yellow, daisylike flowers on 1- to 2½-foot-tall stems. The leaves, which grow basally, are heart-shaped. The plant may go dormant during the summer, especially where temperatures are hot. Varieties include 'Miss Mason' or 'Madame Mason', which retains its foliage better during the summer, and 'Spring Beauty', which has a double flower.

Growing Tips

This plant generally is more successful in the northern portions of its range. Plant Leopard's Bane in partial shade, especially where summers are hot; in cool climates, it will grow in full sun. Soil should be rich, well drained, and moist, even when the plant is dormant. Divide the plant in spring or fall every 2–3 years to avoid having the center of the plant die out.

Epimedium *(Epimedium)*

Zone 5

Also called barrenwort, this plant for the rock garden or ground cover has wiry stems. Its heart-shaped, light green foliage is often tinged with red in spring and fall. Popular species for the garden include Longspur Epimedium *(E. grandiflorum)*, which has flowers of white, yellow, pink, or violet; and Red Epimedium *(E. × rubrum)*, which has bright pink to red flowers. Persian Epimedium (*E. × versicolor*, seen here) has red and yellow flowers. All grow to about 12 inches.

Growing Tips

Plant epimedium in partial shade. These plants tolerate full sun only in cool climates; in hot regions, the foliage will burn in the sun. The soil should be rich and slightly acid. Moist soil is best, but the plants will tolerate dry soil. With a little protection, the foliage may be kept green over the winter; when spring arrives, cut back old stems. These plants may be left undisturbed for many years, but dividing is easy if it proves necessary.

Dropwort *(Filipendula vulgaris)* Zone 4

The tiny white flowers on this species are single; 'Flore Pleno', the variety seen here, has double flowers. The loose clusters bloom in mid- to late summer on leafless stems, 2–3 feet tall, that rise out of very finely cut, fernlike basal foliage. Closely related species are *F. palmata,* Meadowsweet, which has rose-pink flowers; *F. rubra,* Queen-of-the-Prairie, which has magenta flowers; and *F. ulmaria,* or Queen-of-the-Meadow, which has white flowers. All are sometimes sold under the name *Spiraea.*

Growing Tips

All these species do best in very moist garden soil, with the exception of Dropwort, which requires partial shade in rich, dry soil. Members of the genus are easy to increase by division of the clumps in early spring. Dropwort also self-sows.

Galaxy *(Galax urceolata)*

Zone 5

The name of this plant comes from the Greek word *gala,* for "milk"; the flowers are pale white and wispy like the Milky Way. The thin flowering spikes of Galaxy will be nicely set off by ferns and other shade-loving plants in the woodland garden. The spikes of tiny flowers may be up to 12 inches long on thin, 2½-foot-long, leafless stems. The heart-shaped leaves, which grow at the base, are evergreen, turning bronze with age. The species is sometimes sold as *G. aphylla* and has also been known as *G. rotundifolia.* In some areas, the plant escapes cultivation to reestablish itself in the wild.

Growing Tips

Galaxy grows in full to partial shade in moist soil. Optimum growth requires acid soil with abundant organic matter, so add peat moss or compost to enrich the soil. Plants may be increased either by division or by rooting cuttings of the rhizomes (the horizontal underground stems).

Sweet Woodruff *(Galium odoratum)* Zone 5

Sometimes called *Asperula odorata*, Sweet Woodruff grows 6–12 inches tall and spreads to 24 inches across; it is best suited to informal plantings. The white, star-shaped flowers, ¼ inch across, bloom in mid-spring atop stems covered with shiny, whorled leaves. The leaves and stems of this spreading ground cover have been used in flavoring May wine. In medieval times the fragrant blossoms of *G. verum*, a yellow-flowered species, were used to stuff mattresses—giving rise to one name for these plants, bedstraw.

Growing Tips

Plant Sweet Woodruff in partial to full shade in moist, well-drained, slightly acid soil. When grown in too much sun and insufficient moisture, the plants will become stunted and may die down. With the arrival of spring, prune the plant back to prevent it from becoming leggy. In addition, it should also be divided in early spring if the center starts to die out. Winter protection will be beneficial in the northern limits of its hardiness.

Willow Gentian *(Gentiana asclepiadea)* Zones 6–7

Although gentians are well suited to the shady perennial border, they may present a challenge to the gardener. The species shown here, known as Willow Gentian because of the shape of the leaves, is one of the easier gentians to grow. The dark blue flowers are 1½ inches across and bloom in late summer or early fall on 2-foot-tall, arching stems.

Growing Tips

Gentians should be grown in partial shade, especially where summers are hot. Cool, humid growing conditions are critical. Soil should be acid, rich, and moist; mulching will ensure that the soil remains cool and damp. Gentian does not like to be transplanted, so select its site with care. Seeding is the preferred method of propagation, because division generally presents too much of a disturbance.

Cranesbill *(Geranium)*

Zones 4–5

These plants should not be confused with the annual garden geraniums, which belong to the genus *Pelargonium.* Cranesbills are low-growing, spreading perennials with single flowers and divided or lobed leaves. The most common species are *G. dalmaticum,* which grows 6 inches high and has rose-colored flowers; *G. endressii,* Pyrenean Cranesbill, which grows 12 to 18 inches high and has rose-pink flowers; and *G. maculatum,* Wild Geranium, which grows 12 to 20 inches high and has pale lilac flowers. The hybrid 'Johnson's Blue', pictured here, grows 12 inches high and is one of the truest blue flowers for the garden.

Growing Tips

The species mentioned above should be planted in partial shade, especially where summers are hot, in soil that is rich, fertile, moist, and well drained. Cranesbills are easy to grow and are readily increased by division of the clumps in spring or fall.

Hellebore *(Helleborus)*

Zones 4–5

Two hellebores, the Christmas Rose *(H. niger)* and the Lenten Rose (*H. orientalis,* seen here) are similar in appearance, with single, 2- to 3-inch flowers of white, cream, pale pink, or greenish white blooming among evergreen basal foliage. The Christmas Rose is 12 inches tall and blooms in late fall, winter, or very early spring, depending on the locality; the Lenten Rose grows to 18 inches and blooms in early spring. The source of ingredients in many powerful drugs, the root of *H. niger* yields a violent toxin.

Growing Tips

Both the Christmas and Lenten roses prefer partial shade and moist, rich, well-drained soil. They often appear when snow is on the ground and can be protected from damage by snow, ice, and rain by a translucent cover. Provide mulch in summer to keep the soil moist. The roots can be divided in late summer, but you must be careful, because the roots are very brittle. Plants may not bloom for several years after being moved.

Dame's-Rocket *(Hesperis matronalis)* Zone 4

Also called Sweet Rocket, this perennial has phlox-like flowers of purple, lilac, or mauve that bloom in early summer to midsummer. The blooms, which are delightfully fragrant at night, appear on branching plants 2–3 feet tall. There are also forms with double flowers and with white flowers.

Growing Tips

Dame's-Rocket grows in partial shade or full sun. It prefers moist, well-drained, alkaline soil and needs to be heavily fertilized. The species is often a biennial and not long-lived; plants may die out after blooming. Start seeds a season before you expect them to bloom, and replace plants that die with seedlings. If it is allowed to reseed, Dame's-Rocket will often act as a perennial.

Coral Bells *(Heuchera sanguinea)* Zone 4

The species shown here is the most easily cultivated of the alumroots, a group of attractive North American wildflowers. The delicate, airy clusters of these small, bell-shaped summer flowers are perfect for the front of the shady border, in the rock garden, or as a filler. The dark green leaves, which are basal, are round, scalloped, and leathery. The foliage grows in a mound 3–6 inches tall; the flowers appear on wiry stems 12–18 inches tall. The blooms of the species are deep pink to red; there are hybrids with deep red or white flowers.

Growing Tips

Plant Coral Bells in partial shade in rich, fertile, well-drained soil. Full sun is tolerated only in cool climates. These plants prefer moist soil but will tolerate drought; excellent drainage is critical in the winter. When planting, set the crown of the plant above the level of the soil so that it will not rot. When clumps become crowded, they can be easily divided. Winter protection may be necessary in the northern limits of the plant's hardiness.

Hosta *(Hosta)*

Zone 4

Grown chiefly for its rich green basal foliage, hosta—which is also called plantainlily—brings an added bonus in summer, when it sends up graceful spires of white, blue, or lavender flowers. The leaves vary in length from several inches to more than a foot, depending on the species; they come in a range of colors, including green, blue, gold, yellow, and white. Many kinds show variegation or deep texturing. The species most commonly cultivated include *H. lancifolia* (Narrowleaf Plantainlily, shown here); *H. fortunei*, Fortune's Plantainlily, with ribbed leaves; and *H. plantaginea*, with fragrant flowers. There are many cultivars and hybrids as well.

Growing Tips

Most hosta species require partial to full shade, but *H. undulata* will tolerate full sun. Soil should be moist, rich, and well drained, although once it is established, hosta will tolerate drought. Wet soil in winter can damage the plants. Hosta can stay in place for many years without being divided, but can be readily increased by spring or fall division.

Crested Iris *(Iris cristata)*

Zone 4

Most irises demand full sun, but this dwarf gem is one that grows best in partial shade. The flowers, which closely resemble those of the larger irises, may be white, blue, or purple, with a fuzzy yellow crest on the outer petals. They bloom in mid-spring. A valued plant for the rock garden, Crested Iris grows 4–6 inches high and has typical strap-shaped iris foliage. The other major irises that grow in partial shade are the Siberian Iris, *I. sibirica,* and the variety 'Louisiana'.

Growing Tips

Plant Crested Iris in partial shade in rich, moist soil that is acid and well drained. In areas where the soil is constantly moist and temperatures are cool, Crested Iris can be grown in full sun. This species needs division less often than other irises. When dividing the rhizomes (horizontal underground roots), either after the plants have flowered or in late summer, be sure that you replant them on top of the soil and do not cover them.

Spotted Dead Nettle *(Lamium maculatum)* Zone 4

This rapid-growing perennial has spikes of purple, white, or pink flowers on 6- to 12-inch stems in late spring or early summer. The foliage that clothes the square stems may be yellow, green with white or silver markings along the central vein, or silver with a green margin. Seen here is the cultivar 'White Nancy'.

Growing Tips

Plant Spotted Dead Nettle in partial to full shade in any well-drained garden soil; rich, moist soil will give the most vigorous growth. Once established, the plant will withstand considerable drought. It is very aggressive in its growth, but it can be contained by an underground barrier; division in the spring or fall will also keep it under better control. Space plants 18–24 inches apart when replanting.

Rocket Ligularia *(Ligularia × przewalskii)* Zone 4

This perennial lives up to its name—its pointed, 2-foot-tall yellow spikes of flowers atop 4- to 6-foot black stems look like a rocket in flight. Rocket Ligularia blooms in late summer and fall over broad, toothed, triangular to round foliage that makes a decorative mound before the plant comes into bloom. Seen here is the cultivar, 'The Rocket'. Related but quite different looking is *L. dentata,* Bigleaf Goldenray, which bears daisylike orange flowers with brown centers in mid- to late summer. Blooms appear on 4-foot stems over heart-shaped leaves 12 inches across. The variety 'Desdemona' is more compact, with leaves a brownish green above and mahogany-red below.

Growing Tips

Plant Rocket Ligularia in partial shade in rich, moist, well-drained soil. Plants should be divided in spring and the divisions planted 3 feet apart. Bigleaf Goldenray, which must have constantly moist soil, grows well at the sides of streams, ponds, and natural pools.

Blue Lily-Turf *(Liriope muscari)*

Zone 6

Liriope grows in tufts of grassy evergreen foliage that may be dark green or green with yellow or white stripes. The leaves are ½ inch wide; the purple, blue, or white flowers, which resemble grape-hyacinths, bloom in spikes from the center of the arching clump in late summer. Plants reach a height of 12–18 inches, with the stalk of the flower cluster as high as the top of the foliage. The cultivar 'John Birch' is seen here.

Growing Tips

Plant lily-turf in partial to full shade. A fertile, rich, moist, sandy soil is preferred, although the plant will tolerate poor, dry soil. Foliage may become tattered or brown in northern winters. It can be cut to the ground in early spring; when grown in a large expanse, it may be mowed. Lily-turf may also be divided in early spring; set new plants 12 inches apart.

Blue Lobelia *(Lobelia siphilitica)* Zone 5

A good plant for late summer gardens, Blue Lobelia has spikes of bright blue, 1-inch flowers atop 2- to 4-foot stems. A native plant, it is best used in wildflower or woodland gardens. Its cousin, Cardinal-Flower, *L. cardinalis,* has longer spikes of 1½-inch scarlet flowers on stems 3–6 feet tall. Cardinal-Flower is winter hardy to zone 3. Both lobelias are easy to grow and work well in open borders.

Growing Tips·

Plant Blue Lobelia or Cardinal-Flower in partial shade and rich, moist, slightly acid, well-drained soil. They will tolerate full sun if the soil is extremely moist. Both grow well in a waterside setting and self-seed easily. They may need to be staked. The plants produce offsets (short lateral shoots) each year, which can be removed in spring and replanted 12 inches away.

Lupine *(Lupinus)*

Zone 5

Lupines are among the showiest flowers for the late spring garden, and the hybrids known as Russell Lupines, such as the one shown here, are especially fine. Thick spikes of pealike flowers are 18–24 inches long, on 4-foot stems. 'Russell Hybrids' have ½- to 1-inch flowers of white, yellow, pink, red, blue, and purple, with some flowers bicolored. The spikes very often grow in a curled or twisted manner.

Growing Tips

Lupines prefer partial shade but can be grown in full sun in cool climates. Soil must be cool, moist, rich, and well drained; excellent drainage is especially important during the winter. It is essential that the roots be kept cool, so apply a mulch in early spring. Lupines do not grow well in areas with hot, dry summers. Remove spikes as soon as the plants have finished flowering. The deep roots of these plants make them hard to divide or move, but they are easy to grow from seed; nick the seed coat before sowing.

Yellow Loosestrife *(Lysimachia punctata)* Zone 5

The yellow flowers of this perennial appear in the leaf axils in early summer. The plants grow 2–3 feet tall on erect stems. A close relative, *L. clethroides*, is called Gooseneck Loosestrife for the narrow spikes of white flowers at the ends of the stems, which curve gracefully over to the side. It blooms in midsummer on plants 2–3 feet tall. These species, like others in the genus, grow aggressively if not contained and may crowd out other, native plants.

Growing Tips

Plant loosestrife in partial shade in moist, well-drained soil. These species will tolerate full sun in cool regions if the soil is kept constantly moist. They can be divided in spring or fall and replanted 12 inches apart.

Virginia Bluebells *(Mertensia virginica)* Zone 4

The nodding bells on this shade-loving wildflower change color from pink to blue. The 1-inch-long flowers appear in mid-spring on stems 2 feet tall. The cultivar 'Alba' has white flowers. The foliage, which is often spotted, disappears during the summer when the plant becomes dormant.

Growing Tips

Virginia Bluebells grow well under deciduous trees where they have early spring sunshine but partial shade for the rest of the season. Plant them in moist, acid soil that is rich and cool. Mulch in mid-spring to maintain ideal soil conditions. Division is very difficult; it should only be attempted in summer, while plants are dormant. It is easier to increase the plant from seedlings, because the species self-sows readily.

Bee Balm *(Monarda didyma)*

Zone 4

Named for its attractiveness to bees, this species is also a favorite of hummingbirds. Bee Balm has red, purple, lavender, pink, or white flowers that bloom in summer on square, hairy stems 2–3 feet tall. The leaves have a minty scent. Bee Balm grows rapidly, spreading by underground shoots.

Growing Tips

Plant Bee Balm in partial shade. Any good garden soil is acceptable. Divide often in the spring to keep the plants from becoming invasive; space new plants 18–24 inches apart. Underground barriers will also control their rapidly spreading growth.

True Forget-Me-Not *(Myosotis scorpioides)* Zone 5

Most garden forget-me-nots are best treated as hardy annuals or biennials, but *M. scorpioides* is a true perennial and is an attractive ground cover or base for spring-flowering bulbs. The stems are more or less prostrate and 12–18 inches long, creating a mat 15 inches high. The tiny blue flowers have a yellow, pink, or white eye; there is also a pink-flowering form. The species blooms in mid-spring; the variety *semperflorens,* pictured here, blooms until frost but does not grow as tall.

Growing Tips

Plant forget-me-not in partial to full shade. It will tolerate full sun only if the soil is kept extremely moist, in places such as streamsides and pond margins. Soil should be rich and well drained; you must keep it moist at all times. Forget-me-not self-sows readily. Divide in early spring; set new plants 12 inches apart.

Creeping Forget-Me-Not *(Omphalodes verna)* Zone 6

This pretty species is a relative of the True Forget-Me-Not, but there are many visible differences. Both have blue, 5-lobed, spring-blooming flowers, but the flowers of Creeping Forget-Me-Not are larger, to ½ inch across, and borne in looser clusters. This plant also has larger and differently shaped foliage. Creeping Forget-Me-Not has prostrate main stems and erect flowering stems 8 inches high.

Growing Tips

Plant Creeping Forget-Me-Not in full shade in rich, cool, moist, well-drained soil that is slightly alkaline. A mulch applied in early spring will help to maintain proper soil conditions. Divide the roots in spring or fall and plant 12 inches apart.

Creeping Phlox *(Phlox stolonifera)* Zone 4

Creeping Phlox is a rock-garden or edging favorite that grows 10–12 inches high and 18 inches across. The stems, which are covered with oval foliage, root as they creep along the ground. The fragrant flowers bloom in dense clusters in mid-spring; they may be white, pink, rose, lavender, purple, or blue. The cultivar 'Blue Ridge' is seen here. Wild Blue Phlox *(P. divaricata)* is another spreading phlox that grows 12 inches high, with lance-shaped leaves and blue to mauve flowers. Both are closely related to *P. subulata* (also known as Moss Pink, Ground Pink, or Mountain Pink); this species is a lower-growing, sun-loving plant.

Growing Tips

Creeping Phlox likes partial shade in soil that is rich, moist, and slightly acidic. Wild Blue Phlox grows in partial to full shade. Shear plants back after they flower to keep them compact. Divide plants in spring or fall and plant the divisions 12–15 inches apart.

.hinese Lantern-Plant *(Physalis alkekengi)* Zone 5

This perennial takes its name from its ornamental calyx, which turns pale yellow to deep orange or red in the fall. When cut, the "lanterns" can be dried and will last for weeks or even months. The spring-blooming flowers are white and inconspicuous. The Chinese Lantern-Plant grows quickly from long, creeping, underground stems and can become quite invasive. The cutting stem grows to 2 feet tall.

Growing Tips

Chinese Lantern-Plant will grow in any well-drained garden soil in shade or full sun. It will tolerate poor and dry soils. To keep it within bounds, divide and replant it every spring, or install some sort of an underground barrier. The colored calyxes contain seeds; if left on the plant, they will break open and the seeds will easily germinate the following spring. To dry the lanterns, cut them as soon as they turn orange and hang them upside down in an airy, dry spot.

False Dragonhead *(Physostegia virginiana)* Zone 4

Also known as Obedient Plant, False Dragonhead bears 8-inch-long spikes of reddish-purple, rose, pink, or lilac flowers in late summer. 'Summer Snow', a cultivar with white flowers, blooms earlier than the species. False Dragonheads grow to 3–5 feet tall; the spikes make good cut flowers.

Growing Tips

False Dragonhead is easy to grow in partial shade; if you attempt to grow it in full sun, the soil must be kept constantly moist. The species prefers rich, moist, well-drained soil, and can be grown at the water's edge. Plants located in full sun or dry soil will not grow as tall. Clumps increase in size quickly and should be divided every other year in spring or fall to keep them in bounds; space new plants 18 inches from existing plants.

Jacob's Ladder *(Polemonium caeruleum)*

Zone 4

This strong-growing perennial reaches a height of 3 feet and bears clusters of 1-inch blue or purple flowers in late spring or early summer. The leaves have many narrow, lance-shaped leaflets and are arranged on the stems like the rungs on a ladder. There is a variety *album,* with white flowers. The closely related *P. reptans,* Creeping Polemonium, grows 8–12 inches high and has a spreading habit.

Growing Tips

Plant Jacob's Ladder in partial shade or full sun in moist, rich, well-drained soil. When grown in full sun, the plant benefits from afternoon shade. The tips of the leaves will turn brown unless the soil is kept very moist during the summer. Divide the plant in the fall and replant 18 inches apart.

Solomon's-Seal *(Polygonatum odoratum)* Zone 5

Few plants for the mid-spring shady or woodland garden are as graceful as Solomon's-Seal. The arching branches from which the small, bell-shaped, creamy white, fragrant flowers hang grow up to 4 feet long, creating a mound 3 feet high and wide. Seen here is Variegated Solomon's-Seal *(P.o.* var. *thunbergii)*. The variety 'Variegatum' is smaller growing, with white-tipped, white-edged leaves.

Growing Tips

Plant Solomon's-Seal in partial to full shade in rich, acid, moist, well-drained soil. Plants grown in full shade will tolerate dry soil. These plants can be left undisturbed for years. When division of the rhizomes is necessary, do it in early spring and set the plants 2–3 feet apart. Be sure that each division has at least 1 bud eye. Solomon's-Seal will not grow well in areas with warm winters.

ıropean Bistort *(Polygonum bistorta)* Zone 4

Members of this genus are most commonly called fleeceflower for the soft, woolly texture of the flowers. European Bistort has basal leaves that look like paddles and dense, 6-inch-long spikes of pink flowers that bloom on 1½-foot flower stalks in early summer. The cultivar 'Superbum', seen here, grows 2–3 feet high. The stems are angled and have swollen joints like bamboo.

Growing Tips

Plant European Bistort in partial shade in rich, moist, well-drained soil. In cool areas, it will grow in full sun. European Bistort will be more aggressive in poor soil. If flowers are cut back after they bloom, the plant may bloom again in late summer. Divide the fleshy roots in early spring and set the plants 12–18 inches apart.

Primrose *(Primula)*

Zones 5–6

Primroses should be a part of every spring shade garden. They are valued for their colorful flowers that bloom in clusters or whorled spikes. They have round or oblong leaves that are often textured. *P. helodoxa,* Amber Primrose, has interrupted clusters of flowers along an 18- to 36-inch stem. *P. japonica,* Japanese Primrose, has round heads of purple, pink, or white flowers on 8- to 16-inch stems. *P.* × *polyantha,* Polyanthus Primrose, is a group of hybrids with rounded clusters of flowers in every color of the rainbow. Cowslip Primrose (*P. veris,* seen here) has nodding clusters of fragrant yellow flowers with orange centers on 6- to 8-inch stems. *P. vulgaris,* the English Primrose, has yellow or blue flowers.

Growing Tips

Primroses do best in partial shade in rich, moist soil that is fertile, slightly acid, and well drained. These plants prefer cool, humid climates. Primroses are short-lived, but frequent division after flowering can extend their life. Set plants 12 inches apart.

Blue Lungwort *(Pulmonaria angustifolia)* Zone 4

Useful in borders, Blue Lungwort is a spreading plant that grows 6–12 inches tall and 12–18 inches across. The 1-inch flowers, which bloom in late spring and early summer, are blue, opening from pink buds. The creeping roots grow rapidly but do not become overly invasive. Other garden lungworts include *P. longifolia,* which grows 12 inches tall and has blue flowers, and *P. saccharata,* Bethlehem Sage, which grows to 14 inches tall and has white or reddish-purple flowers.

Growing Tips

Plant Blue Lungwort in partial to full shade in cool, rich, moist, well-drained soil. A mulch applied in mid-spring will help to maintain the proper soil conditions. Lungwort may be divided in summer after the plant has finished blooming. Space new plants 12 inches apart and water them well until they become established.

Sage *(Salvia)*

Zones 6–8

Few gardeners realize that this group of plants, which includes the annual salvia and the herb sage, will grow well in partial shade. *S. azurea,* Blue Sage, is a graceful, open plant with ½- to ¾-inch deep blue flowers that bloom in late summer and fall. Without pinching, the plants will grow 5–6 feet tall; with pinching until early summer, they can be kept to 3 feet. The variety *S.a. grandiflora,* Pitcher's Salvia, is seen here; it is similar, with larger flowers. Meadow Clary *(S. pratensis)* grows to 3 feet; it has bright blue flowers and aromatic foliage.

Growing Tips

Plant sage in partial shade; in cool climates, it can be grown in full sun. Soil should be light, sandy, slightly fertile, and well drained. Salvia does not like excessive moisture around its roots, especially in winter. In spring, divide carefully as it may do poorly after transplanting. Space plants 18 inches apart.

Great Burnet *(Sanguisorba canadensis)* Zone 4

Also called American Burnet, this strong-growing perennial reaches 3–6 feet in height and has compound leaves at the base of the plant. The white flowers are small and bloom in numerous 6- to 8-inch spikes on thin stems. Plant Great Burnet where color is needed in late summer through fall; it does especially well in the shady wildflower garden or near streams or bogs. This plant is listed in some books and catalogues as *Poterium canadense.*

Growing Tips

Plant Great Burnet in partial shade or sun in rich, slightly acid soil that is kept evenly moist. Divide roots in the spring or fall or propagate by seeds. Space new plants 18–24 inches apart.

Strawberry Geranium *(Saxifraga stolonifera)* Zone 6

This trailing plant is also called "Mother of Thousands," because of the many plantlets that form at the ends of runners. The hairy, round, scalloped foliage with white veins and red undersides forms a mat 4–5 inches high. The white flowers bloom on 6- to 12-inch stems in early summer. Strawberry Geranium is most attractive in a hanging basket where the runners with their plantlets can cascade over the sides of the container.

Growing Tips

Strawberry Geranium grows best if it receives morning sun and afternoon shade. In hot areas, partial to full shade should be provided all day. Soil should be sandy, slightly alkaline, and well drained. Plants can be divided in spring, or the plantlets removed from the runners and rooted.

ecrop *(Sedum)* Zone 4

The stonecrops are a large group of succulent plants that may have either an upright or trailing habit. Tiny flowers bloom in clusters at the ends of the stems. The upright forms include Showy Stonecrop *(S. spectabile),* 2 feet tall with pink fall flowers, and 'Autumn Joy', 2 feet high with pink blooms darkening to rust in fall. The trailing forms include October Daphne *(S. sieboldii,* seen here), which grows to 6 inches high and produces pink flowers in late fall; *S. acre,* 2 inches high with yellow spring flowers; Orange Stonecrop *(S. kamtschaticum),* 12 inches tall with yellow flowers in late summer; and Two-row Stonecrop *(S. spurium),* 6 inches tall with pink to red flowers in mid- to late summer. Depending on their habit, stonecrops are grown in borders or as ground covers.

Growing Tips

The stonecrops mentioned here will grow in partial shade in sandy, dry, infertile, well-drained soil. Good drainage is critical in the winter. They can be easily divided in early spring. Leaves and stems root easily.

Oconee Bells *(Shortia galacifolia)*

Zone 5

Although extremely rare in the wild, this native North American species does well in gardens where summers are mild. The 1-inch, white-fringed flowers bloom in early summer to midsummer; the blossoms and the attractive, shiny green and bronze leaves make this a good choice for the shady rock garden. Plants spread by underground stems.

Growing Tips

Plant Oconee Bells in partial or full shade in acid, cool, moist soil that is rich and well drained. A mulch applied in mid-spring will help to maintain the proper soil conditions. Oconee Bells does not grow well where summer temperatures are very high. It can be divided in early spring but does not transplant well, so choose its permanent site with care and divide infrequently.

False Solomon's-Seal *(Smilacina racemosa)* Zone 4

The foliage of this plant resembles that of true Solomon's-Seal: broadly lance-shaped with obvious parallel veins. The greenish-white flowers, however, are easily distinguished—blooming in feathery branching clusters 4–6 inches long at the tops of erect, 3-foot-tall stems. The blossoms of the False Solomon's-Seal are fragrant and bloom in late spring. Red berries follow the flowers in late summer; they are edible but bitter.

Growing Tips

Plant False Solomon's-Seal in partial to full shade in moist, rich, slightly acid soil. A thin layer of leaf mulch will be beneficial in retaining moisture and keeping the soil cool. False Solomon's-Seal does not grow well in areas where summers are very hot. Divide the thick rhizomes in the fall; space divisions 12–18 inches apart.

Celandine Poppy *(Stylophorum diphyllum)* Zone 6

Like other poppies, Celandine Poppy has flowers with 4 petals that bloom in late spring over deeply cut, lacy foliage. The 2-inch blooms are either deep yellow or red and may appear in small clusters. Plants reach a height of 18 inches. This species works well in the wildflower garden.

Growing Tips

Plant Celandine Poppy in partial shade in rich, moist, well-drained soil. It self-seeds readily and can become very invasive, so it will need to be thinned out yearly. Plants can be divided in fall and replanted 12 inches apart.

Russian Comfrey *(Symphytum × uplandicum)* Zone 5

Grown in the herb garden for use in teas, Russian Comfrey is also a very attractive plant for the perennial border. The species can grow to 6 feet tall but usually does not exceed 2–3 feet. The blue flowers that appear in nodding clusters are 1 inch long and bloom early in the summer.

Growing Tips

Plant Russian Comfrey in partial shade or full sun in moderately rich, slightly acid, moist, well-drained soil. The species has a deep tap root and does not transplant well. To propagate it, divide the roots in spring or fall into 1-inch segments and replant these 3 feet apart. To harvest leaves for tea, pick them when the plants start to flower and dry them in a spot with good air circulation.

Meadowrue *(Thalictrum)*

Zones 5–6

Although the flowers of Meadowrue are small, they are showy because they bloom in large, often branching clusters. Columbine Meadowrue, *T. aquilegifolium,* is 2–3 feet tall and has lavender, purple, pink, orange, or white flowers in early summer. Lavender Mist Meadowrue (*T. rochebrunianum,* shown here) is 3–5 feet tall and has purple to pink flowers that bloom in mid- to late summer. Dusty Meadowrue, *T. speciosissimum,* is 3–5 feet tall and has yellow flowers in midsummer. All have compound leaves.

Growing Tips

Meadowrue prefers partial shade, especially where summers are hot. Soil should be rich, moist, and well drained. The taller species will need staking. All can be divided in spring and should be replanted 12–18 inches apart.

Spiderwort *(Tradescantia × andersoniana)* Zone 5

Spiderwort resembles the related houseplant, Wandering Jew. Its stems are jointed, weak, and juicy. The 1-inch-wide, summer-blooming flowers, which have 3 petals, are white, pink, red, purple, or blue and last only a day. The plant can reach a height of 24 inches but falls over after flowering; it can be cut back to produce a neater clump. Cultivars show much improvement over the species; they include 'Pauline' (seen here), with large pink flowers, and 'Zwaanenberg Blue', which has large blue flowers. Spiderwort is sometimes sold as *T. virginiana*.

Growing Tips

Spiderwort grows best in partial to full shade, although it also tolerates full sun. It should have rich, moist, soil that is acid and well drained. Plants are easy to divide in spring; stems may also be detached at a joint and will root easily. Space plants 18 inches apart.

Toad Lily *(Tricyrtis hirta)*

Zone 6

This spreading perennial grows 3 feet tall and has oval, hairy foliage on arching branches. The bell-shaped flowers are 1 inch long and white on the outside, but so heavily spotted on the inside with purple and black that they look purple. The flowers appear in small clusters in the leaf axils and at the branch tips in mid-fall.

Growing Tips

Plant Toad Lily in partial shade in rich, acid, fertile soil that is kept moist. Mulch with leaves in spring to ensure that the soil stays cool and moist. Divide in spring when growth starts if necessary, replanting 18 inches apart. The flowers are not showy from a distance, so situate plants where they can be seen at close range with other fall-blooming plants.

Snow Trillium *(Trillium grandiflorum)* Zone 5

Also called Wakerobin (because it blooms in early spring, when the robin starts to sing), Snow Trillium grows 12–18 inches tall and has 2- to 3-inch flowers on 3-inch stems. The waxy flowers are white and fade to pink as they age. There are double-flowered forms available. There are several other *Trillium* species that may do well in the woodland garden; one of the showiest, Purple Trillium, has large purple blooms that are unfortunately malodorous and attractive to flies.

Growing Tips

Snow Trillium grows best in cool climates in partial to full shade. The soil must be slightly acid, deep, rich, well drained, and constantly moist. Where conditions are right, the species will self-sow readily and form attractive colonies. It also spreads by rhizomes. Divide the plants in late summer and space them 12–18 inches apart.

Globeflower *(Trollius)*

Zones 5-

As the name implies, these plants have globe-shaped flowers; they bloom in mid-spring. Common Globeflower, *T. europaeus,* has 1- to 2-inch double yellow flowers. Ledebour Globeflower, *T. ledebourii,* has 2-inch orange flowers with globe-shaped outer petals and petal-like stamens in the center; the cultivar 'Golden Queen', seen here, has large yellow flowers. Both species grow 2–3 feet tall and have coarsely toothed, deeply lobed leaves.

Growing Tips

Globeflower is easy to grow in cool areas and requires rich, moist, boggy soil. It is good for sunken gardens and at the edges of water gardens, although it will grow in a flower border if given similar conditions. Plant in partial shade. Divide plants in the fall and replant them 18 inches apart; plants grow slowly, and frequent division will not be necessary. Remove fading or spent flowers to prolong the blooming period.

on Valerian *(Valeriana officinalis)* Zone 5

Also called Heliotrope, this species is valued as a garden plant for its clusters of fragrant white, pink, red, lavender, or blue to purple flowers, which bloom in summer. The bushy plant grows 3–4 feet tall and has lance-shaped or fernlike leaves. Because it has a tendency to spread, Common Valerian grows best in a wildflower garden. It makes a good cut flower.

Growing Tips

Common Valerian is easy to grow and is not fussy about growing conditions. Plant in partial shade or full sun in average, well-drained garden soil. It may be divided in spring or fall; space new plants 18–24 inches apart.

Culver's Root *(Veronica virginica)*

Zone 4

The speedwells, to which group this plant belongs, are a large genus of herbs that do well in the rock garden and along borders. Some speedwells are attractive flowering prostrate plants, good for ground cover or edging; others are tall-growing species. Shown here is the cultivar *V. virginica* 'Rosea', which grows from 2–6 feet tall. It bears pink flowers, ⅛ inch across, in a spikelike cluster 6–8 inches tall. The species is similar, with white flowers. It is sometimes sold as *Veronicastrum virginicum.*

Growing Tips

Culver's Root is easy to grow in average, well-drained soil. Plant in partial shade or sun. The species is also easy to increase by division, which should be done after the plant has bloomed in late summer.

Violet *(Viola)*

Zone 5

This perennial relative of the garden pansies bears 5-petalled flowers and grows to 8 inches high over basal foliage. Horned Violet (*V. cornuta,* seen here) has flowers 1½ inches across that may be violet, white, apricot, red, or yellow. It blooms in spring and will stay in bloom all summer where it is cool, if faded flowers are picked. Sweet Violet, *V. odorata,* has fragrant purple, white, or lavender flowers 1 inch wide; the blooms appear in mid-spring. Johnny-Jump-Up *(V. tricolor)* has tricolored blooms of violet, yellow, and white in spring.

Growing Tips

Plant violets in partial shade in rich, moist, fertile, well-drained soil. They grow best in cool climates and benefit from a mulch applied in mid-spring. Winter protection is needed in the northern limits of their hardiness. Where conditions are favorable, they self-sow readily. Sweet Violet sends out long runners that form new plants at their ends. Horned and Sweet violets may also be divided in the spring.

APPENDICES

Map: Paul Singer

HARDINESS ZONE MAP

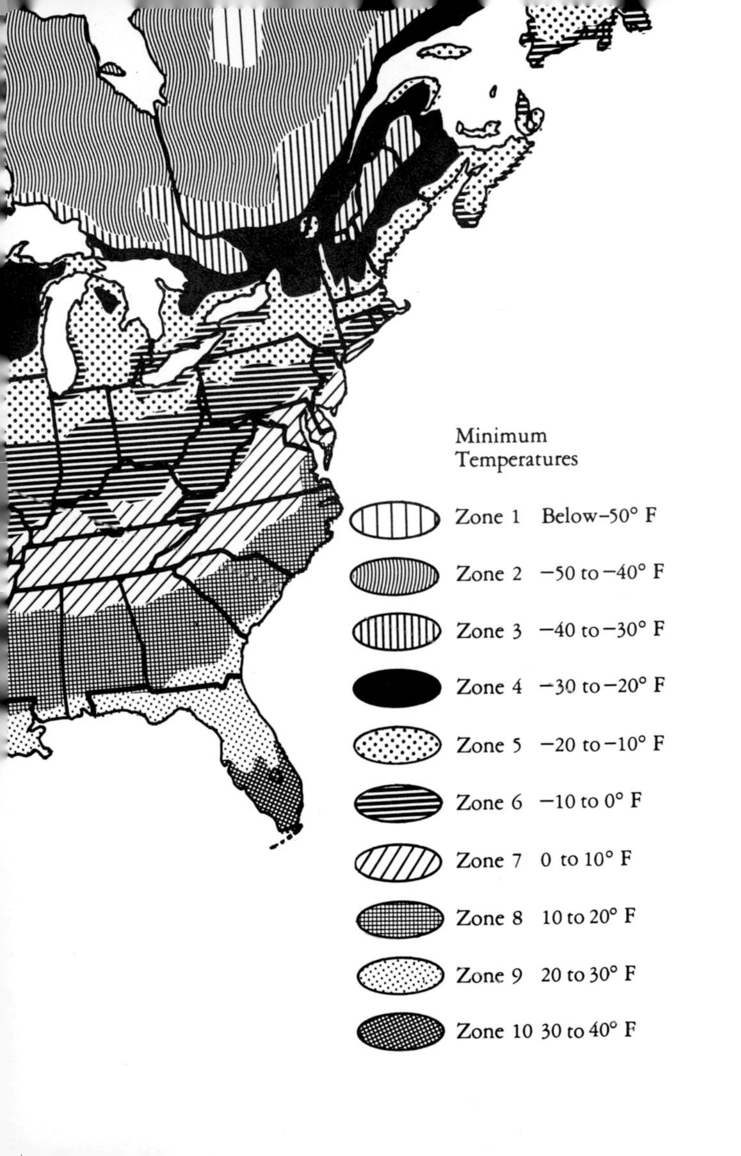
Minimum
Temperatures
Zone 1 Below–50° F
Zone 2 –50 to –40° F
Zone 3 –40 to –30° F
Zone 4 –30 to –20° F
Zone 5 –20 to –10° F
Zone 6 –10 to 0° F
Zone 7 0 to 10° F
Zone 8 10 to 20° F
Zone 9 20 to 30° F
Zone 10 30 to 40° F

GARDEN PESTS AND DISEASES

PLANT PESTS and diseases are a fact of life for a gardener. Therefore, it is helpful to become familiar with common pests and diseases in your area and to learn how to control them.

Symptoms of Plant Problems

Because the same general symptoms are associated with many diseases and pests, some experience is needed to determine their causes.

Diseases

Both fungi and bacteria are responsible for a variety of diseases ranging from leaf spots and wilts to root rot, but bacterial diseases usually make the affected plant tissues appear wetter than fungi do. Diseases caused by viruses and mycoplasma, often transmitted by aphids and leafhoppers, display such symptoms as mottled yellow or deformed leaves and twisted or stunted growth.

Insect Pests

Numerous insects attack plants. Sap-sucking insects—including aphids, leafhoppers, and scale insects—suck plant juices. The affected plant becomes yellow, stunted, and misshapen.

Aphids and scale insects produce honeydew, a sticky substance that attracts ants and sooty mold fungus growth. Other pests with rasping-sucking mouthparts, such as thrips and spider mites, scrape plant tissue and then suck the juices that well up in the injured areas.

Leaf-chewers, namely beetles and caterpillars, consume plant leaves, whole or in part. Leaf miners make tunnels within the leaves, creating brown trails and causing leaf tissue to dry. In contrast, borers tunnel into shoots and stems, and their young larvae consume plant tissue, weakening the plant. Some insects, such as various grubs and maggots, feed on roots, weakening or killing the plant.

Nematodes

Microscopic roundworms called nematodes are other pests that attack roots and cause stunting and poor plant growth. Some kinds of nematodes produce galls on roots, while others produce them on leaves.

Environmental Stresses

Some types of plant illness result from environment-related stress, such as severe wind, drought, flooding, or extreme cold. Other problems are caused by salt toxicity, rodents, birds, nutritional deficiencies or excesses, pesticides, or damage from lawn mowers. Many of these injuries are avoidable if you take proper precautions.

Controlling Plant Problems

Always buy healthy disease- and insect-free plants, and select resistant varieties when available. Check leaves and stems for dead areas or off-color and stunted tissue. Later, when you plant your flowers, be sure to prepare the soil properly.

Routine Preventives

By cultivating the soil routinely you will expose insects and disease-causing organisms to the sun and thus lessen their chances of surviving in your garden. In the fall be sure to destroy infested or diseased plants, remove dead leaves and flowers, and clean up plant debris. Do not add diseased or infested material to the compost pile. Spray plants with water from time to time to dislodge insect pests and remove suffocating dust. Pick off the larger insects by hand. To discourage fungal leaf spots and blights, always water plants in the morning and allow the leaves to dry off before nightfall. For the same reason, provide adequate air circulation around leaves and stems by spacing plants properly.

Weeds provide a home for insects and diseases, so pull them up or use herbicides. But do not apply herbicides, including "weed-and-feed" lawn preparations, too close to flower beds. Herbicide injury may cause leaves to become elongated, strap-like, or downward-cupping. Spray weed-killers when there is little air movement, but not on a very hot, dry day.

Insecticides and Fungicides

protect plant tissue from injury due to insects and diseases, mber of insecticides and fungicides are available. However, few products control diseases due to bacteria, viruses, and mycoplasma. Pesticides are usually either "protectant" or "systemic" in nature. Protectants keep insects or disease organisms away from uninfected foliage, while systemics move through the plant and provide some therapeutic or eradicant action as well as protection. Botanical insecticides such as pyrethrum and rotenone have a shorter residual effect on pests, but are considered less toxic and generally safer for the user and the environment than inorganic chemical insecticides. Biological control through the use of organisms like *Bacillus thuringiensis* (a bacterium toxic to moth and butterfly larvae) is effective and safe.

Recommended pesticides may vary to some extent from region to region. Consult your local Cooperative Extension Service or plant professional regarding the appropriate material to use. Always check the pesticide label to be sure that it is registered for use on the pest and plant with which you are dealing. Follow the label concerning safety precautions, dosage, and frequency of application.

GLOSSARY

Acid soil
Soil with a pH value of 6 or lower.

Acute
Pointed.

Alkaline soil
Soil with a pH value of more than 7.

Annual
A plant whose entire life span, from sprouting to flowering and producing seeds, is encompassed in a single growing season. Annuals survive cold or dry seasons as dormant seeds. See also Biennial and Perennial.

Axil
The angle formed by a leafstalk and the stem from which it grows.

Basal leaf
A leaf at the base of stem.

Beard
A fringelike growth on a petal, as in many irises.

Berry
A fleshy fruit, with one to many seeds, developed from a single ovary.

Biennial
A plant whose life span extends to two growing seasons, sprouting in the first growing season and then flowering, producing seed, and dying in the second. See also Annual and Perennial.

Blade
The broad, flat part of a leaf.

Bract
A modified and often scalelike leaf, usually located at the base of a flower, a fruit, or a cluster of flowers or fruits.

Bristle
A stiff, short hair on a stem or leaf.

Bud
A young and undeveloped leaf, flower, or shoot, usually covered tightly with scales.

Bulb
A short underground stem, the swollen portion consisting mostly of fleshy, food-storing scale leaves.

Calyx
Collectively, the sepals of a flower.

Clasping
Surrounding or partly surrounding the stem, as in the base of the leaves of certain plants.

Compound leaf
A leaf made up of two or more leaflets.

Corm
A solid underground stem, resembling a bulb but lacking scales; often with a membranous coat.

Corolla
Collectively, the petals of a flower.

Corona
A crownlike structure on some corollas, as in daffodils.

Creeping
Prostrate or trailing over the ground or over other plants.

Crest
A ridge or appendage on petals, flower clusters, or leaves.

Cross-pollination
The transfer of pollen from one plant to another.

Crown
That part of a plant between the roots and the stem, usually at soil level.

Cultivar
An unvarying plant variety, maintained by vegetative propagation or by inbred seed.

Cutting
A piece of plant without roots; set in a rooting medium, it develops roots, and is then potted as a new plant.

Dead-heading
Removing blooms that are spent.

Deciduous
Dropping its leaves; not evergreen.

Disbudding
The pinching off of selected buds to benefit those left to grow.

Disk flower
The small tubular flowers in the central part of a floral head, as in most members of the daisy family. Also called a disk floret.

Division
Propagation by division of crowns or tubers into segments that can be induced to send out roots.

Double-flowered
Having more than the usual number of petals, usually arranged in extra rows.

Drooping
Pendant or hanging, as in the branches and shoots of a weeping willow.

Evergreen
Retaining leaves for most or all of an annual cycle.

Everlasting
A plant whose flowers can be prepared for dried arrangements.

Fall
One of the sepals of an iris flower, usually drooping. See also Standard.

Fertile
Bearing both stamens and pistils, and therefore able to produce seed.

Floret
One of many very small flowers in a dense flower cluster, especially in the flower heads of the daisy family.

Fruit
The mature, fully developed ovary of a flower, containing one or more seeds.

Genus
A group of closely related species; plural, genera.

Germinate
To sprout.

Herb
A plant without a permanent, woody stem, usually dying back during cold weather.

Herbaceous perennial
An herb that dies back each fall, but sends out new shoots and flowers for several successive years.

Horticulture
The cultivation of plants for ornament or food.

Humus
Partly or wholly decomposed vegetable matter; an important constituent of garden soil.

Hybrid
A plant resulting from a cross between two parent plants belonging to different species, subspecies, or genera.

Invasive
Aggressively spreading away from cultivation.

Lateral bud
A bud borne in the axil of a leaf or branch; not terminal.

Layering
A method of propagation in which a stem is induced to send out roots by surrounding it with soil.

Leaf axil
The angle between the petiole of a leaf and the stem to which it is attached.

Leaflet
One of the subdivisions of a compound leaf.

Loam
A humus-rich soil containing up to 25 percent clay, up to 50 percent silt, and less than 50 percent sand.

Lobe
A segment of a cleft leaf or petal.

Midrib
The primary rib or mid-vein of a leaf or leaflet.

Mulch
A protective covering spread over the soil around the base of plants to retard evaporation, control temperature, or enrich the soil.

Naturalized
Established as a part of the flora in an area other than the place of origin.

Neutral soil
Soil that is neither acid nor alkaline, having a pH value of 7.

Node
The place on the stem where leaves or branches are attached.

Offset
A short, lateral shoot arising near the base of a plant, readily producing new roots, and useful in propagation.

Peat moss
Partly decomposed moss, rich in nutrients and with a high water retention, used as a component of garden soil.

Perennial
A plant whose life span extends over several growing seasons and that produces seeds in several growing seasons, rather than only one. See also Annual and Biennial.

Petal
One of a series of flower parts lying within the sepals and next to the stamens and pistils, often large and brightly colored.

Petiole
The stalk of a leaf.

pH
A symbol for the hydrogen ion content of the soil, and thus means of expressing the acidity or alkalinity of the soil.

Pistil
The female reproductive organ of a flower, consisting of an ovary, style, and stigma.

Pollen
Minute grains containing the male germ cells and released by the stamens.

Propagate
To produce new plants, either by vegetative means involving the rooting of pieces of a plant, or by sowing seeds.

Prostrate
Lying on the ground; creeping.

Raceme
A long flower cluster on which individual flowers each bloom on small stalks from a common, larger, central stalk.

Ray flower
A flower at the edge of a flowerhead of the daisy family, usually bearing a conspicuous, straplike ray.

Rhizomatous
Having rhizomes.

Rhizome
A horizontal underground stem, distinguished from a root by the presence of nodes, and often enlarged by food storage.

Rootstock
The swollen, more or less elongate stem of a perennial herb.

Rosette
A crowded cluster of leaves; usually basal, circular, and at ground level.

Runner
A prostrate shoot, rooting at its nodes.

Seed
A fertilized, ripened ovule, almost always covered with a protective coating and contained in a fruit.

Sepal
One of the outermost series of flower parts, arranged in a ring outside the petals, and usually green and leaflike.

Solitary
Borne singly or alone; not in clusters.

Spathe
A bract or pair of bracts, often large, enclosing the flowers, as in members of the Arum family.

Species
A population of plants or animals whose members are at least potentially able to breed with each other, but which is reproductively isolated from other populations.

Spike
An elongated flower cluster; individual flowers lack stalks.

Stamen
The male reproductive organ of a flower, consisting of a filament and a pollen-containing anther.

Standard
The upper petal or banner of a pea flower; also, an iris petal, usually erect. See also Fall.

Sterile
Lacking stamens or pistils, and therefore not capable of producing seeds.

Subspecies
A naturally occurring geographical variant of a species.

Taproot
The main, central root of a plant.

Terminal bud
A bud borne at the tip of a stem or shoot, rather than in the axil of a leaf. See also Lateral bud.

Terminal raceme
A raceme borne at the tip of the main stem of a plant.

Terminal spike
A spike borne at the tip of the main stem of a plant.

Throat
The opening between the bases of the corolla lobes of a flower, leading into the corolla tube.

Toothed
Having the margin shallowly divided into small, toothlike segments.

Tuber
A swollen, mostly underground stem that bears buds and serves as a storage site for food.

Tufted
Growing in dense clumps, cushions, or tufts.

Variegated.
Marked, striped, or blotched with some color other than green.

Variety
A population of plants that differ consistently from the typical form of the species, either occurring naturally or produced in cultivation.

Vegetative propagation
Propagation by means other than seed.

horl
oup of three or more leaves or shoots, all emerging from at a single node.

PHOTO CREDITS

Sonja Bullaty and Angelo Lomeo ©, Cover, 2, 25

Pamela J. Harper, 26, 27, 28, 29, 31, 32, 33, 35, 36, 37, 38, 39, 40, 41, 42, 43, 44, 45, 47, 48, 50, 52, 55, 56, 57, 58, 60, 61, 62, 63, 64, 65, 66, 69, 71, 72, 74, 76, 77, 80, 81, 83, 84, 85, 87, 88, 89, 90, 92, 94, 95, 96, 97, 99, 101, 102, 103

John A. Lynch, 93, 100

Joy Spurr, 51, 54, 68, 91

Steven M. Still, 30, 34, 46, 49, 53, 59, 67, 70, 73, 75, 78, 79, 82, 86, 98, 104

INDEX

CHANTICLEER PRESS

STEWART, TABORI & CHANG

Publisher
ANDREW STEWART

Senior Editor
ANN WHITMAN

Production
KATHY ROSENBLOOM
KARYN SLUTSKY

Design
JOSEPH RUTT